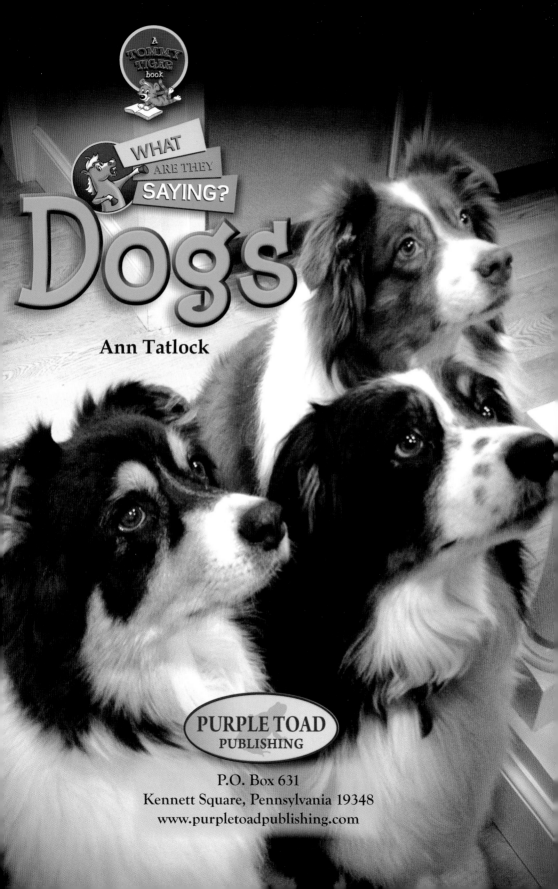

A TOMMY TIGER book

WHAT ARE THEY SAYING?

Dogs

Ann Tatlock

PURPLE TOAD
PUBLISHING

P.O. Box 631
Kennett Square, Pennsylvania 19348
www.purpletoadpublishing.com

Printing   1   2   3   4   5   6   7   8   9

WHAT ARE THEY SAYING?

Birds
Cats
Dogs
Guinea Pigs
Horses

Publisher's Congress-in-Publication Data
Tatlock, Ann
   What Are They Saying: Dogs / Ann Tatlock
     p. cm. — (What are they saying?)
Includes bibliographic references and index.
ISBN: 978-1-62469-034-1 (library bound)
1. Dogs — Juvenile literature.   I. Title.
 SF426.5 2013
 636.7 — dc23
                                                      2013936069

eBook ISBN: 9781624690358

ABOUT THE AUTHOR: Ann Tatlock is author of ten novels. Her works have received numerous awards, including the Silver Angel Award from Excellence in Media and the Midwest Book Award. She lives in the Blue Ridge Mountains of Western North Carolina with her husband, daughter, three Chihuahuas, and a guinea pig named Lilly.

PUBLISHER'S NOTE: The data in this book has been researched in depth, and to the best of our knowledge is factual. Although every measure has been taken to give an accurate account, Purple Toad Publishing makes no warranty of the accuracy of the information and is not liable for damages caused by inaccuracies.

Printed by Lake Book Manufacturing, Chicago, IL

WHAT ARE THEY SAYING?

Dogs

I am stretched out on the floor in a warm ray of sunshine. Since early morning, I have been very busy barking, eating, playing, and napping. Now it is time for the best moment of the day!

Pet Fact:

There are many different breeds of dog.
Mixed breeds—sometimes called mutts or
mongrels—often make the best pets.

Listen! I lift my head, and my ears stand straight up. I hear the school bus stop in front of the house. I hear footsteps on the sidewalk. Someone opens the front door and calls my name. "Charlie!"

6

Pet Fact:

While dogs can't tell time, they have "internal clocks" that let them know when it's time for supper or when to expect their owners home.

"Here I am!" I say, though it sounds like "Yip yip!" My tail wags so fast my whole body dances. My best buddy calls it my Happy Dance.

Pet Fact:

A dog who is about to bite may wag its tail too, but its body will be rigid and its tail pointing up.

I lick my buddy's cheek, which is how I say, "Welcome back! I missed you!"

Pet Fact:

Dogs are very loyal to their owners and offer them a lot of affection.

Now it's my turn for a little loving. I roll over to let my buddy rub my tummy.

Pet Fact:

When a dog offers you its belly, it means it trusts you.

We go to the kitchen, where my buddy has a snack. "Don't forget me!" I say, but it sounds like "Yawp!" My friend smiles. "Sit," he says. I sit. He rewards me with a dog biscuit.

Pet Fact:

With patient training, dogs can master many tricks, such as sitting up to beg, shaking paws, and rolling over.

We go outside, where my buddy picks up a stick. "Ar-owl-wowl-wowl!" I say. "Let's play!" I wait for him to throw the stick, and then I fetch it.

Pet Fact:

A dog makes a moaning sound of happiness when something it really likes is about to happen.

Pet Fact:

A dog whimpers or yelps when it is in pain.

I run across the yard. Suddenly I cry out, "Yelp!" I have stepped on a sharp pebble in the grass. But I am very brave. I keep on running to fetch the stick.

Next my buddy grabs my leash and I know we're going for a walk! "Arff! Arff!" Before we're even out of the yard, I am panting and my tongue is hanging out. "Let's go!"

But wait! First I have to stop and smell everything. I explore my world with my nose.

Pet Fact:

A dog's sense of smell is 100 times stronger than yours!

23

Pet Fact:

Dogs like to roll on the ground to pick up the scent of other animals. They think it smells good, like canine (doggie) perfume!

When I smell something especially interesting, I roll in the grass until my buddy tugs at my leash and tells me to stop.

I'd better be careful because sometimes when I roll on the ground, my buddy puts me in the tub and washes me clean with soapy water. That always makes me shiver because I don't like the water.

Pet Fact:

Grooming your dog includes bathing it, brushing its fur, and keeping its nails clipped.

We walk and walk. It feels good to exercise and stretch my legs. A little dog walks toward us with her buddy. I must seem very big to her. She cowers with her tail between her legs.

With my front legs stretched forward and my wiggling rear end up in the air, I invite her to play. She knows I'm saying, "Let's be friends!"

Look at that dog across the street. He is soooo big! Now I'm the little guy. Just to be safe, I think I'll scamper away and scurry toward home. "Arrrf! Come on, buddy!"

Pet Fact:

Dogs come in four sizes—small (sometimes called toy), medium, large, and giant.

At night, I am happy to curl up beside my best buddy's bed. He reaches over and scratches my ear. "Good night, Charlie," he says. "I love you." I sigh contentedly and close my eyes. It is good to be home. Good night.

Books

Boynton, Sandra. *Doggies.* New York: Little Simon Publishing, 1984.

Day, Alexandra. *Good Dog Carl.* New York: Little Simon Publishing, 1996.

Gravett, Emily. *Dogs.* Douglas, Isle of Man: Pan Macmillan, 2009.

Priddy, Roger. *My Big Animal Book.* New York: St. Martin's Press, 2002.

Schindel, John. *Busy Doggies! A Busy Animals Book.* Berkeley, CA: Tricycle Press, 2003.

Van Fleet, Matthew. *Dog.* New York: Simon & Schuster, 2007.

Works Consulted

Bain, Terry. *You Are a Dog: Life Through the Eyes of Man's Best Friend.* New York: Harmony Books, 2004.

Davis, Caroline. *Essential Dog: The Ultimate Guide to Owning a Happy and Healthy Pet.* London: Octopus Publishing Group Ltd., 2006.

Fogle, Bruce. *Dog Owner's Manual.* New York: Dorling Kindersley, Inc., 2003.

Fogle, Bruce. *Dog: The Definitive Guide for Dog Owners.* Buffalo, NY: Firefly Books Inc., 2010.

Millan, Cesar. *A Member of the Family: Cesar Millan's Guide to a Lifetime of Fulfillment with Your Dog.* New York: Harmony Books, 2008.

On the Internet

Bender, Amy. Top Ten Signs a Dog May Bite
http://dogs.about.com/od/safetytips/tp/top-signs-a-dog-may-bite.htm

Coren, Stanley, PhD. Psychology Today, "Canine Corner"
http://www.psychologytoday.com/blog/canine-corner/

Cute Home Pets
www.cutehomepets.com

Dogs on About.com
http://dogs.about.com/

Duncan, Deb. Come, Sit, Stay . . .Canine Etiquette
www.thedogspeaks.com

Pet Place
www.petplace.com

INDEX